Preludes and Offertories for Piano Solo

Gail Smith

WWW.MELBAY.COM

Table of Contents

O Store Gud

Dedicated to Melinda Poulos

Swedish Folk Song
arranged by Gail Smith

5
5
3
3
3
4
1

5
4
1
1
9
LH
LH
6
tr
9
LH
LH
rit.

A Mighty Fortress is Our God

Dedicated to Alexis Ann Poulos

Martin Luther
arranged by Gail Smith

rit.
cresc.

All Glory, Laud and Honor

St. Theodulph c. 820

Melchior Teschner, 1615
arranged by Gail Smith

cresc.

8va
p

rit.

Doxology

Thomas Ken , 1637-1710
Louis Bourgeois
arranged by Gail Smith
Majestic
f
mf

3
3
3
3
3

When Morning Gilds the Sky

LAUDES DOMINI

Dedicated to Nannette Goodwin

Joseph Barnby, 1838-1896
arranged by Gail Smith

pp

The God of Abraham Praise

Thomas Olivers
based on Jewish Doxology

Synagogue Melody
arranged by Gail Smith

mp
cresc.
p
f
mf
rit.

O God Our Help in Ages Past

Psalm 90
Isaac Watts, 1674-1748

Dedicated to Peggy Pearson

William Croft, 1678-1727
arranged by Gail Smith

f

mp
5
4
2
1
2
1
2
4
5
1
2
3
1
2
3
5
f

rit.

Amazing Grace

John Newton, 1779

Traditional American Melody
arranged by Gail Smith

mf

3

This page has been left blank to avoid awkward page turns

Brethren, We Have Met to Worship

Dedicated to Betty Jane Ruckman

George Atkins

William Moore
arranged by Gail Smith

mf

mf
mf
a tempo
rit.
f
mp

3
rit.
mf
8va
rit.

Come Every Soul by Sin Oppressed

Dedicated to Lynae Katterjohn

John Stockton, 1887

John Stockton
arranged by Gail Smith

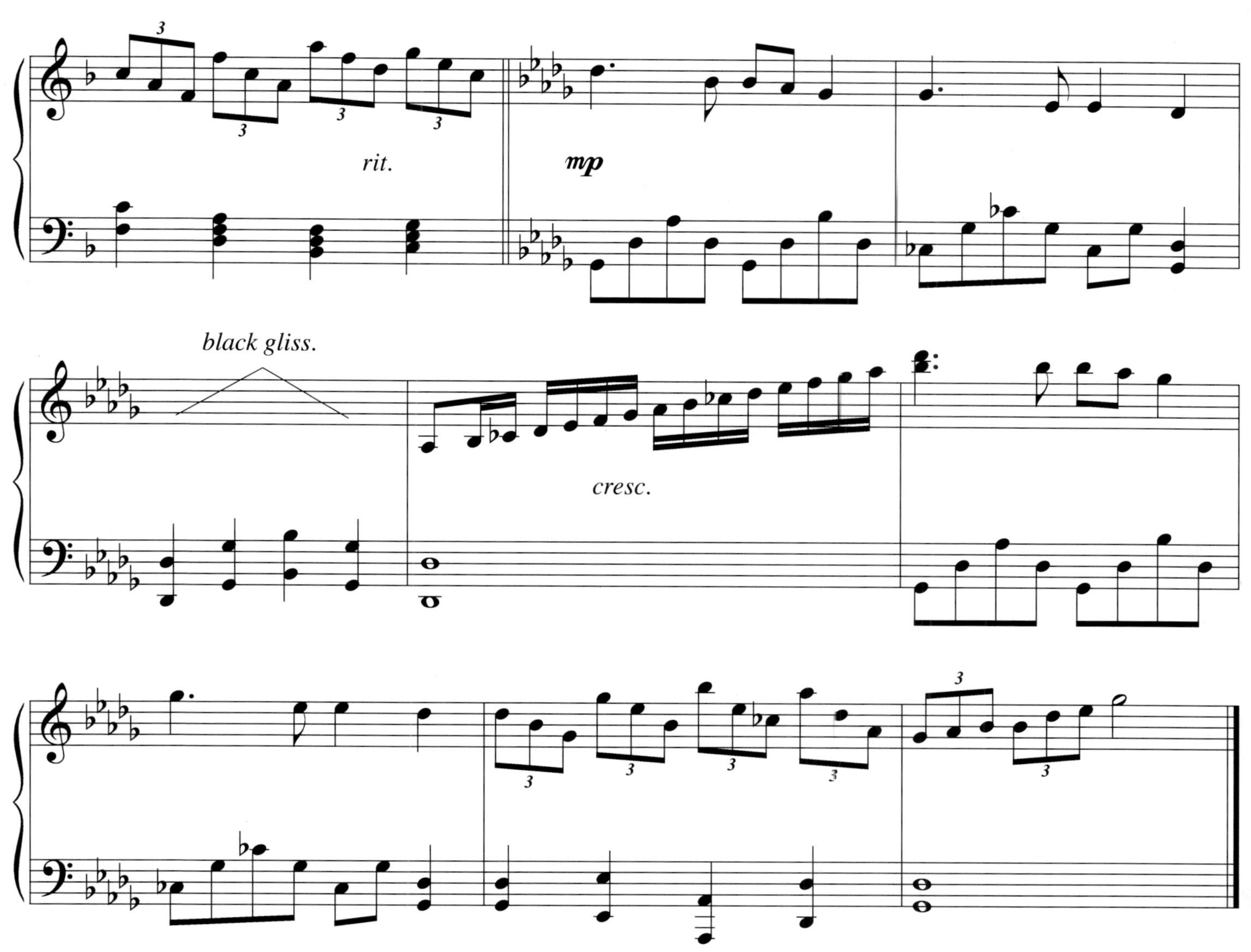
rit.
mp
black gliss.
cresc.

This page has been left blank to avoid awkward page turns

Come, Ye Sinners, Poor and Needy

Joseph Heart, 1759

American Melody
arranged by Gail Smith

I Have Decided to Follow Jesus

Dedicated to Alex Hall

Folk melody from India
arranged by Gail Smith

mf
rit.

How Firm a Foundation

Traditional American Melody
Caldwells Union Harmony, 1837
arranged by Gail Smith

trem.
trem.
trem.
trem.

There is a Fountain

arranged by Gail Smith

rit.
p

What Can Wash Away My Sin

Dedicated to Ruth Pearce

Robert Lowry, 1876

Robert Lowry
arranged by Gail Smith

mf
mf
6
3
3
3
3
rit.

This page has been left blank to avoid awkward page turns

Jesus Tender Shepherd, Hear Me

To my granddaughter, Erika Hall, born June 25, 1998

Charlotte Barnard
arranged by Gail Smith

Gentle Lullaby

Open My Eyes, That I May See

Clara H. Scott, 1896
arranged by Gail Smith

Give of Your Best to the Master

Dedicated to Djina Sterling

Mrs. Charles Barnard
arranged by Gail Smith

mf

rit.
a tempo
p

This page has been left blank to avoid awkward page turns

Beyond the Sunset

Blanche Brock
arranged by Gail Smith

Jesus Saves

William J. Kirkpatrick
arranged by Gail Smith

Moderato

mf

rit.

a tempo

f

rit.

My Hope is Built

Dedicated to Gwen Larkin

William Bradbury
arranged by Gail Smith

D.C. al Fine

Wonderful Words of Life

Dedicated to Dawn Reed Tate

Philip P. Bliss
arranged by Gail Smith

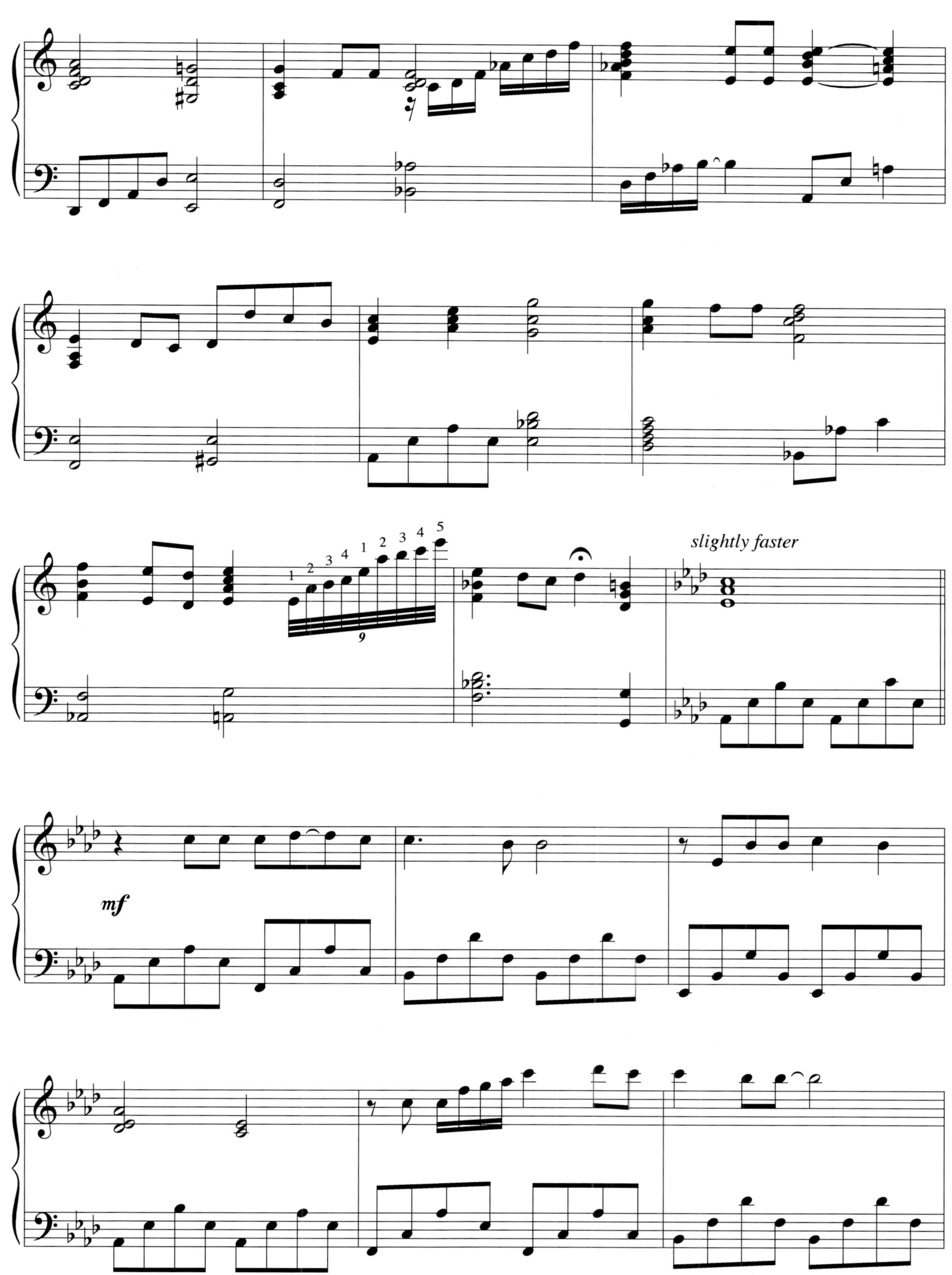
slightly faster
mf

mp

Marvelous Grace

Daniel Towner, 1911
arranged by Gail Smith

rit.

rit.

At the Cross

Dedicated to K. C. Rice

Ralph E. Hudson
arranged by Gail Smith

rit.

Turn Your Eyes Upon Jesus

Helen Lemmel
arranged by Gail Smith

12
rit.

Must Jesus Bear the Cross Alone?

George N. Allen
arranged by Gail Smith

3
3
3
3
3
3
3
3
3
3

Battle Hymn of the Republic

arranged by Gail Smith

America the Beautiful

This page has been left blank to avoid awkward page turns

My Country Tis of Thee

arranged by Gail Smith

The Star-Spangled Banner

Dedicated to Jesse Adam Yancoskie

Francis Scott Key
arranged by Gail Smith

Simple Gifts

arranged by Gail Smith

mf

p

rit.

We Gather Together

Dedicated to Alyssa Katterjohn

Netherlands Folk Song
arranged by Gail Smith

Joy to the World

Dedicated to Nathan Smith

George Fredrick Handel
arranged by Gail Smith

Six Variations on

Jesus Loves Me

Introduction

arranged by Gail Smith

Maestoso

f *p* *mf* 8va 15 *cresc.*

Variation in E Flat

1 2 3 4 1
3 2 1 4 3 2 1 3
3 4 3 2 1 2 1 4
3 4 3 2 1 2 1 3
1 2 3 4 1
3 2 1 4 3 2 1 3

Variation in C

Variation in D

Variation in G

Variation in G Minor

Variation in D Flat

Variations on

O Worship the King

arranged by Gail Smith

Theme

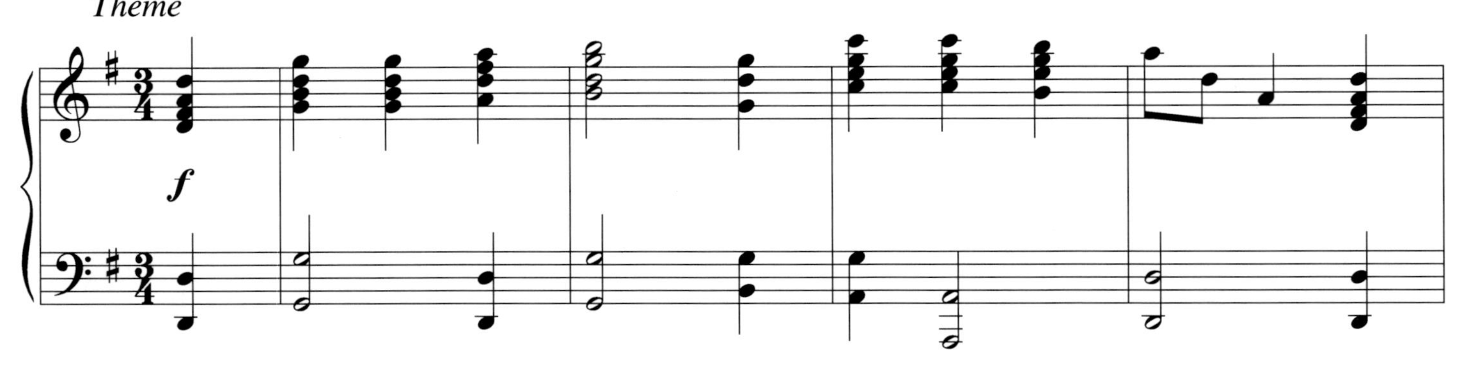

O Worship the King

With Melody in Left Hand

arranged by Gail Smith

O Worship the King

Ballad Tempo

O Worship the King

rit.

O Worship the King
Variation No. 5
In the Style of Early Blues
arranged by Gail Smith
Slow
mf

O Worship the King

In the Ragtime Style of Scott Joplin

arranged by Gail Smith

rit.

O Worship the King

Near to the Heart of God

Dedicated to Adina Stone

C. B. McAfee
arranged by Gail Smith

Moderato

mf

Slower

rit.

rit.
p
3
rit.
decresc.
p

All Hail the Power

Dedicated to Canaan Bellinghausen

James Ellor
arranged by Gail Smith

Allegretto

mf

cresc.

f

10

This page has been left blank to avoid awkward page turns

O That Will Be Glory
Dedicated to Anne Kennedy
Charles Gabriel
arranged by Gail Smith
Moderato
mf

rit.

RH
RH
LH

He Lives

Alfred H. Ackley
arranged by Gail Smith

rit.

I Surrender All

Winfield S. Weeden
arranged by Gail Smith

rit.

3
3
3
rit.
3
3
3
3
3
3
3
3

Now Thank We All Our God

Johann Cruger
arranged by Gail Smith

rit.

Guide Me, O Thou Great Jehovah

John Hughes
arranged by Gail Smith

Moderato

mf

Joy to the World

Alternate Version

George Fredrick Handel
arranged by Gail Smith

3
Ped.
f

rit.

O Come, O Come, Emmanuel

Dedicated to Sarah Heaton

Latin Hymn
arranged by Gail Smith

8va
LH

About the Author

Gail Smith was born in Bridgeport, Connecticut, on January 26, 1943. Gail's father, Carl Erick Johnson, sang tenor in the church choir. Her mother, Ethel, played the piano and had Gail start piano lessons.

Smith received her Bachelor of Fine Arts Degree from Florida Atlantic University. She has taught piano students from the age of 3 to 96! Her blind student, Ivan, was seen on national TV. Giving musical lecture recitals by portraying the composer's wife has been an effective way to reach audiences with the history of music. Gail has portrayed Marian MacDowell and Anna Magdalena Bach. She gives many workshops and concerts throughout the United States as well as in Germany and Japan.

Smith's life has revolved around her family, church and music. She is the pianist of the famed Coral Ridge Presbyterian church. She has been active in many organizations including being national Music Chairman of the National League of American Pen Women and is a former president of the Broward County branch. Ms. Smith is also a member of The Freedoms Foundation of Valley Forge, National Music Teachers Association, and Federation of Music Clubs.

Ms. Smith's works include many piano solos, choral works, a piano trio, a composition for four pianists and numerous vocal solos. She has arranged hundreds of hymns, Indian melodies, and folk tunes from many countries. Her trademark is her piano palindromes, which can be played backwards as well as forwards and sound the same.

Alphabetical Index

Other Mel Bay Sacred Piano Collections

WWW.MELBAY.COM